My Journey
With Cancer

My Journey With Cancer

You can survive and even thrive

H. Deloris Jones

Copyright © 2019 by H. Deloris Jones.

ISBN: Softcover   978-1-7960-4618-2
          eBook   978-1-7960-4617-5

All rights reserved. No part of this book may be reproduced or transmitted in any form or by any means, electronic or mechanical, including photocopying, recording, or by any information storage and retrieval system, without permission in writing from the copyright owner.

The views expressed in this work are solely those of the author and do not necessarily reflect the views of the publisher, and the publisher hereby disclaims any responsibility for them.

Scripture quotations marked KJV are from the Holy Bible, King James Version (Authorized Version). First published in 1611. Quoted from the KJV Classic Reference Bible, Copyright © 1983 by The Zondervan Corporation.

Unless otherwise indicated, all scripture quotations are from The Holy Bible, English Standard Version® (ESV®). Copyright ©2001 by Crossway Bibles, a division of Good News Publishers. Used by permission. All rights reserved.

Scripture quotations marked NIV are taken from the Holy Bible, New International Version®. NIV®. Copyright © 1973, 1978, 1984 by International Bible Society. Used by permission of Zondervan. All rights reserved. [Biblica]

Any people depicted in stock imagery provided by Getty Images are models, and such images are being used for illustrative purposes only.
Certain stock imagery © Getty Images.

Print information available on the last page.

Rev. date: 07/16/2019

To order additional copies of this book, contact:
Xlibris
1-888-795-4274
www.Xlibris.com
Orders@Xlibris.com
798736

CONTENTS

Foreword ix
Introduction xiii

Chapter 1   When the Doctor Says You Have Cancer 1
Chapter 2   How to Meditate on Healing Thoughts 9
Chapter 3   How to Be Your Own Advocate 17
Chapter 4   Treating Your Body as a Temple 21
Chapter 5   Changing Your Eating Habits 27

Food for Thought 33
Scripture to Meditate on Daily 35

I would like to dedicate this book to my five children and all my grandchildren,

George Lee II, Tracy Lanice, Marvin Antonio,
Jermaine Danyel, and Shawn Enrico.

After sharing the news with my youngest
son, he called the family together
to tell them that I had just been diagnosed
with cervical cancer. They all came
over to his house, joined hands, and put me
in the middle and began to pray.
"They continued to pray."

Later, my oldest son George and his son Geo
flew from California to visit.
I love you all and I'm so glad God chose me to be your mother.
You've always been very loving children
and
I'm so very proud of you.
Also, I'm thankful to my pastor, Angelo O. Jones, and my church
family for their continuous prayers.

To a special friend, Lorraine Johnson,
who I met many years ago, who came to the hospital and
stayed all day until I got out of recovery.

Foreword

You are a woman who shows herself as open, unashamed, and fearless in bearing herself in the Gospel. I admire your spirit of helping others for them to experience the power of the Lord Jesus Christ through your eyes.

Your willingness to expose areas of your life that show He can transform people's lives, no matter where they begin, is admirable.

I know this book will impact so many as they continue through their challenges in life. But more than that, this book will show them that through your victory, they too can find theirs.

You are truly a woman I admire.

— Marja Lee Freeman

Prayer for Your Journey

Father, I pray that You give them strength
For today
That they trust and depend on
You
Even though they may become
Fearful
Along this journey
Let them known that You are with them
That
You will guide them into Your presence
And that
You will restore their health
Release
All toxicities from every organ and cell

In Jesus's name.
Amen.

Introduction

I'm writing this book because I want you people to know that God can pull you through any situation, even though you get fearful and frightened. Also, God will bring people in your path if you pray and ask for His guidance.

This is the third time I've started writing this book, and I almost lost everything I typed; but luckily I had saved some of it in Google Docs. We all seem to have a hard time with change in our lives. Season changes all the time, and there is nothing we can do about it. And just like the seasons' change, we have to change too. But we are kicking and fighting change all the time.

It takes work on our part to stay healthy or become healthy. It doesn't happen overnight; and because of it, we tend to give up and throw in the towel, and eventually stop trying to win the battle. But if you're consistent and persistent, you can overcome obstacles that are keeping you from staying focused on your journey toward becoming healthy.

I've struggled also with staying focused on eating less processed foods practically all of my young adult life, and of course, I really didn't eat healthy foods in my childhood. I would actually eat potato chips and french fries for breakfast a lot of times on the way to school. Eating healthy is not a losing battle. Start one day at a time, and you will get there.

Another thing most of us are worried or stressed about is our daily lives. How we are going to pay the bills piling up on the kitchen table or stressed about our jobs of not having a job, about raising our child or children . . . and so on. I truly believe stress causes a lot of our illness.

I meet people who say they haven't had a vacation for twenty years or more. Most of the time, we need to recover from taking a vacation, especially if we travel out of town more than six hours.

The problem we have is that we don't know how to relax our minds. The reality is the brain never stops letting thoughts run through our minds . . . most of us don't know how to relax and have a "just for me day."

We try to please everyone we deal with on a day-to-day basis because everyone wants our undivided attention. Sometimes, we just have to say "wait a minute, time out," and take a few deep breaths, and let them know when you have time to listen to them.

Here are some tips to just to relax your mind:

(1) Go for a long walk and take time to see the beauty that is over your heart, the beautiful sky and the bright sunlight that's giving you energy, the beautiful differently colored flowers, and of course, the beautiful trees. Don't forget to listen to the birds singing and the breeze blowing in your hair.
(2) Take a long nap.
(3) Join a gym that is inexpensive.
(4) Stay hydrated, drink plenty of water. We really don't have time to actually experience the present moment God has given us. The very air we breathe comes from Him. We take for granted that we will see the next day.
(5) Why not take a train to see the free museums that are available in your area?
(6) Take a weekend off and ask a friend to go with you to the beach.

Also, we need to keep as much stress out of our lives as much as possible. Only you know when there is too much stress and you need to put on the brakes. No one can do this for you. Also, know that your emotions play a large part of your body breaking down and becoming ill.

We're holding a lot of guilt, shame, and unforgiveness in our hearts, and we have to let go of these if we want to be well and live, not just breathe, but live a guilt-free and exciting life full of joy and peace. We need to take the time to really enjoy spending time with family and friends. I forgot to mention restful sleep is very vital, and drinking at least four to five glasses of water a day, even eight if you can.

You can't take everything to heart—how someone treats you or what they say to you. Get away from people who consistently say negative things about you and other people. I order for your body to stay strong and healthy; you have to give your spirit what it needs. Your spirit cannot survive in a weak body. Your spirit needs to be nourished, just like your body needs the right foods. You need to read the Word of God to keep your spirit strong. There are a lot of inspirational books and CDs you can purchase to help you keep your spirit fed.

You need to know how much God wants you well. His word says, "He will never leave you nor forsake you," (Heb. 13:5).

There is a constant fight going on every day in your mind, body, and soul. Your spirit tells you this is not good for you, but your body says, "I need this, I got to have this." The gut feeling says you know this isn't good for you, but you do it anyway.

Chapter 1

When the Doctor Says You Have Cancer

Here is where I begin my story. I began to spot like I was having my menstrual period and I had stopped having menstruation seven years ago. I didn't have medical insurance, but I had signed up with a company who paid 60–70 percent of your doctor bill depending if you went to one of their doctors.

Well, I found Dr. DeSandes, and I made an appointment with his office, and I was diagnosed as having a bladder infection, so he prescribed an antibiotic, but after two weeks I was still spotting, so he sent me to Fairfax Radiology to get a sonogram. The sonogram revealed that my uterus was enlarged. So then I was scheduled for a D and C at Alexandria Hospital. After waiting for two weeks for the result, Dr. DeSandes called me in to discuss the results.

He came in my rooms singing "It's Me Oh Lord."

He said, "Young lady, you have cancer." I became numb and I was speechless. I didn't know what to say. I had to take a deep breath. He said one thing, "I want you to do is not worry about your doctor bills or anything. Just concentrate on getting well." By the way Dr. DeSandes is a Christian. He said, "I'm going to send you to this specialist, who's a good friend of mine, and he and his team of doctors work at a free clinic and I'm making an appointment for you to see him right away."

God was truly ordering my steps. This free clinic was only ten minutes from where I lived.

I finally met Dr. John Elkas, at his office in Fairfax, not far from INOVA Fairfax Hospital. After reviewing my test, he said "This is a mean cancer but you're a healthy young woman."

When I met Dr. Elkas, it looked like there was a halo around his head, like the picture of an angel and I know it wasn't my imagination.

So I had to wait until doctor Elkas had a conference with his team of doctors. After that his team of doctors had a talk with my family on how they would proceed with my treatment plan.

Dr. Elkas's office called me to schedule surgery on August 23, 2012. My daughter and granddaughter Chada drove me to Fairfax Hospital. Dr. Oliver, who was a female doctor, assisted Dr. Elkas, along with his other team of medical professionals.

After my operation, I only stayed overnight and I was discharged later that day. My granddaughter stayed with me all night, that's how much she loves her grandmother. I had to show the nurses I could wall around the corridor without any trouble and I did. I did eat breakfast before I left the hospital, I hadn't eaten bacon in years, but I was so hungry, I'll tell you what I ate for breakfast. I had three scrambled eggs, oatmeal, three slices of bacon, toast, and coffee.

My sister asked me to stay with her for a week because she knew it would be painful for me to go up and down stairs. It was nice to be waited on for a while considering I was still in a lot of pain.

The pain medication was keeping me so drowsy that every time I would go to the bathroom I would fall asleep on the toilet and my sister would have to wake me up, so I decided to stop taking it and resort to Tylenol or just bear with the pain. She also said I could even get addicted to the medication after seeing the opioids epidemic; I'm sure glad I listened to her.

I didn't begin chemo right away because Dr. Elkas and his team of doctors had to have a conference before I could start treatment. I was given a treatment plan and a paper that listed all the side effects. I didn't read the list because I didn't want to be looking for them, even if one of them showed up. One of the side effects was that I would be experience nausea. But I never have had nausea, thank God. I did experience my mouth being raw but not for long. I was informed by a friend to gurgle with baking soda and salt water.

Before starting chemo, my daughter took me to the Vitamin Shoppe to get the powered green drink with lots of vitamins and minerals. Also, we purchased mushroom supplements and vitamin D with 2000 mg. The supplement MACCA is very good for your immune system. After a round of chemo, we need to replenish our cells; just a regular meal would not be enough. We have to get the nutrients from our fresh fruits and vegetables to sustain us, not coffee, tea, and a slice of cake.

Chemo depletes a lot of our required nutrients that our cells need in order to survive. I also added fresh vegetables in my juicing, such as cucumbers, celery, and sometimes beets. You can do this at least three times a week.

It has occurred to me that bad eating habits start in the womb. Your mother and maybe your father had something to do with it also; whatever you consume does affect your unborn child.

We hold years and years of toxicity in our organs as well as our cells. Our cells also have memory of trauma and of course our brain records and keeps record of everything, good and bad.

Our body is so amazing. God our Creator designed our bodies to heal itself, but of course we have our part to play. We are constantly gaining new cells. Peaceful rest or may I say, sleep, is so important as well as hydrating our bodies with water that's not diluted with coffee, teas, or sodas. If you need to make it more tasty, add lemon, lime, or fresh orange slices in a pitcher or large container. Make sure you walk at least thirty minutes a day and get some sunshine, a good source of vitamin D.

Medication does not heal the body; if it did, you wouldn't have to take it for years and years. Just like a car needs water, gas, and oil to perform. We need fresh food and water, a clear and focused mind, and meditate on the Word of God to keep us strong. Listening to meditation music will help calm your mind to release peace in your everyday journey.

My daughter would take me to my 7:00 a.m. treatment where I would sit almost three hours to have chemo with other cancer patients. I did experience my white blood cells being low, which was considered very dangerous. This also meant that if I got a temperature of 99.9 or 100 F, I had to go to the hospital and get checked. Usually I was admitted.

Because of having the medical terminology neutropenia, I was consistently in and out of the hospital. One time I was given two pints of blood because of my white blood cells. These cells are important because it has to do with your helping to decrease the risk of infection in your body.

I also got a blood clot in my right arm, but because I was in so much pain, I assumed it came from taking chemo. I was told that it was possibly because of the port that was implanted in my upper chest. I also had to have medication for it. I had to give myself an injection every night at the same time, because other medications didn't work for me.

> *Death and life are in the*
> *power of the tongue and they that*
> *love it shall eat the fruit thereof.*
> *(Prov. 18:21, KJV)*

So if you love life and want to live a healthy life, you will not say negative words out of your mouth, you will speak good things over your life, such as "I am well," "My mind is healthy," "I am not sick." Even though you are under attack by the devil, who goes around as a lion seeking whom he may devour, you say "I can overcome it." He comes to rob, steal, and kill everything in your life that is good, but you cannot let him in your thoughts and your heart. Tell him he cannot have your life because you belong to God, and God says He will give you life and that more abundantly. His word says you have to declare it, but you will see the glory of the Lord, Amen.

> *The thief cometh not, but for to*
> *steal and to kill, and to destroy. I am come*

that you might have life, and that they might have it more abundantly.
(John 10:10, KJV)

You have the power, which means you are capable of much more than you think. You can't let life just beat you up without opening your mouth. The best medicine in the world is laughter. I was looking at TV and this man said he was diagnosed with cancer. He decided to buy comedy movies and he laughed his way to wellness. He probably didn't realize how powerful laughter was until the doctor told him he no longer had cancer. This alone changed the course of his life. We tend to let everything stress us out. Our relationships with people, we don't understand, people that don't have our best interest at heart. We feel like we have to please people in our life, people who have no desire to please us nor even care about us. Sometimes it's all about them and what makes them happy. Let us remember, we all have our own purpose in this world. Therefore, we must seek to find out what's our purpose.

A lot of us just go to work, maybe church and back home to our families if we're married. Sometimes, we live, barely trying to make ends meet.

We all need recreation in our life, which is not a part of most of our lives because we don't take the time to actually breathe.

Some of us go to church and not even participate. Most of the time we're watching the clock, which I'm guilty of sometimes, even though I do praise and worship.

We all need to take time to have fun. Some people haven't had a vacation in years simply because they really can't afford it. And sometimes, some people feel guilty if they take some leisurely time off work, believe it or not.

We definitely need to spend time walking in the park, looking at the beautiful creation that God has made for us—the beautiful trees and flowers, the stars and moon; listening to the wind blowing the leaves on the trees, the birds singing, even the bees and the butterflies.

Also you need time out, whether you're married or single. It's important that you take time out for yourself. You need time to replenish your mind, your emotions, and your soul, to improve your health. It's important for you and your family to know more about what you're feeling and also what they are feeling, because you're not on this journey by yourself. Your love ones are being affected also, and I'm sure they want the best for you as well.

I believe having the right nutrients in your body will improve your immune system.

If you can, I suggest you eat less meat at this time. No more than two times a week. *No red meat at all* because it takes a long time to digest for one thing. I suggest chicken and fish. Lots of fresh fruits, vegetables, and nuts. No bacon not even turkey bacon. Again I suggest you leave sugar alone for a while such as candy, pies, and cakes. Cancer thrives on sugar. Once you finished chemo, you need to know what you can take. It's at your discretion, I'm merely making a suggestion. I do know sugar lowers your immune system.

I don't like to say *diet* because you now should begin to make eating wholesome food a part of your lifestyle. Therefore, it's not considered a diet but a lifestyle. Most of us crave for sugar but we must remember not to go overboard. Also watch your sodium intake.

Don't keep on your mind what you're going through. Relax continue doing the things you like to do. Try to still enjoy doing fun things with your family. Get your mind off yourself. Know that you're going to be okay and tell yourself "I'm going to get through this, I'm going to be fine." God has you in the palm of his hand and he's on this journey with you.

> *And the LORD, it is he that doth go*
> *Before thee; he will be with thee, he will not fail thee,*
> *Neither forsake thee; fear not, neither be dismayed.*
> *(Deut. 31:8 KJV)*

I pray that you have a good support group such as family and friends. I do realize that some people aren't very personal and don't trust other people's input. That's why you should try to get as much information as you possibly can. Of course, you can't take everyone's advice. I trust at least two doctors' nutritional advice. One is Dr. Furhman and Dr. Axe. They basically suggest that you cook your food at home and eat out as less as possible, especially if you're going through chemo and radiation.

There are a lot of genetically modified organism (GMO) foods in the market in the market, or foods created in a laboratory. Go on Google and research. Your main concern is to keep a positive attitude and also get in touch with your spirituality, which needs to be fed as well as your natural body. I don't know if you believe in God or what people call a Higher Being. It's time to reach out and make choices that will help you to maintain your inner peace.

Look at your life and see if you have people lifting you up or pulling you down. Not everyone believe God is a healer. You have to continue to stay around positive people. You have to get a healthy network of support because we all need each other, but someone toxic in your life will result in a negative effect, and will show up in your health sooner or later.

We need to reach out to people who can sow positive affirmations in our lives. We have to talk good to our mind out loud for our ears to hear and our hearts to become one.

We're not kind to our bodies. We don't rest when we need to. I believe that's why we're unbalanced. We need to learn how to live balanced lives. When we have a headache and feel sick, instead of taking time to go to a quiet place and just do some conscious breathing, we reach for Advil or Tylenol. Ask yourself, "Why is my head hurting, what's really going on in my body. Did I give myself enough to drink or did I get enough sleep, which could be affecting me right now." The majority of us, including me, think about medication.

We are spirit beings also, that why in the proceeding chapters I will give you scriptures from the Holy Bible to feel your spirit man in order to thrive, so you can mediate on them. Also there is music in which you can mediate to bring a calmness to your life. Taking the time out of your busy schedule to read a book as well as the Bible will begin to bring much calmness and joy to your existence, while you're on this journey.

The minute you feel anxious, stop what you're doing and focus on what you're thinking about. Nine times out of ten, it's not even your thoughts. If you're spiritual at all, you will find you need to pull down strongholds that are attacking your mind. Joyce Meyers is the author of several books that I recommend that you read, such as *Battlefield of the Mind*.

We go through a lot of challenges in our life; it actually can make us a stronger person, depending on how we perceive it. A lot of our problems are emotional. Our bodies reacts to situations we're going through. We let other people control our emotions. An example, we could have a boss that's getting on our last nerve, sooner or later that's going to affect you physically if you can't let it go. We've have all experienced trauma in our lives from time to time; ever since childhood and some of the trauma we went through is still affecting us, we have to forgive and let it go. Release the stress, the hurt, and pain of yesterday.

Chapter 2

How to Meditate on Healing Thoughts

First things first. I had to learn how to put God first in my life. I didn't realize I wasn't putting him first. I really didn't know what it meant to put him first. You have to talk to him to develop a relationship with him, like you would do a wife or a husband. When you're in relationship, you want the person to talk to you on a daily basis. You want to know and feel that they love you. God wants the same thing from us. I try to start my day with thanking God for waking me up this morning and by asking him to order my steps, and let me accomplish what I need to do for that day to stay on track. I ask him for protection and guidance and to protect my family, friends, and love ones from danger.

"No one is immune to cancer or any disease."

Even though we see a lot of socializing on social media, people are not really communicating effectively with each other. Most families don't sit down at the dinner table and while eating, they're mostly on their phones communicating with other people. Parents aren't able to get through to their children, they take to heart what the social media is saying, what they should wear, how they should act. There's bullying going on among the children and parents are the last to know, *people we have to wake up.*

Cancer is not the only sickness that's taking us out. We have to get back to what matters the most. For one thing we're eating more fast foods, and that's causing a lot of diseases, even though it shows up years later. Our food industries need to be looked into more carefully, children need healthy food in order to think properly and to get and maintain good grades. I know I've gotten a little off track about meditating, but who can meditate with improper nutrition. Your brain cannot function properly when you're not getting good nutrition. That's a fact, and I don't have to prove it either.

I received in the mail from Daystar Television healing scriptures from Dodie Osteen, when there was no cure for her liver cancer and the doctor sent her home and said there was nothing else they could do for her. There was no treatment. She basically stood on the Word of God for her healing. She said she actually stood on her Bible and she and her husband began to confess the Word of God for her healing. Every prescribed medication have at least three to five pages of side effects.

You can call Daystar at *800-329-0029* and order your healing CD and the book of scriptures written by Dodie Olsteen. I'm sure it's still in print so you can order them. It's food for the soul. These are some of the healing scriptures I will like to share with you. Because Jesus died on the cross for our sins, and by His stripes we are healed, every time they whipped Him it opened up a wound which is known as a stripe and he bore thirty-nine stripes and they took care of every category of sickness. He did this because He loved us and because He loved His Father; He died to pay the price for our sins even though we didn't deserve it, but He loved us so.

John 3:16, KJV
For God so loved the world that he gave his only begotten son that whosoever believe in him shall not perish but shall have eternal life.

Deuteronomy 30:19, KJV
I call heaven and earth to record this day against you, that I have set before your life and death, blessings and cursing: therefore choose life, that both thou and thy seed may live.

So now that you know you should choose life, you have the power in you to live, no matter what's attacking your body. You have a choice. Take that choice.

Mark 11:24, KJV
Therefore I say unto you. What things soever ye desire. When we pray believe that ye receive them, and ye receive them, and ye shall have them.

Healing should be the desires of your heart, because I'm sure you want to live, but in a healthy body, soul and spirit.

Isaiah 55:11, NIV
So shall my word be that goeth forth out of my mouth, it shall not return unto me void, but it shall accomplish that which I please, and it shall prosper in the thing whereto I sent it.

My words shall heal me. I will not waiver. I will believe that I am healed and everything I say shall come to pass, because God has heard my prayer and I believe he loves me and that he is my Father that is in Heaven.

Hebrews 4:15, KJV
For we have not a high priest which cannot be touched with the feelings of our infirmities; but was in all points tempted like as we are yet without sin.

Jesus was touched by our infirmities because he went about healing all that were sick and even raised people from the dead. I believe sometimes we're holding unforgiveness of others and even ourselves in our hearts. We need to search our souls and ask for forgiveness and even forgive.

Psalm 42:11, KJV
Why are thou cast down, O my soul? And why art thou disquieted within me? Hope thou in God: for I shall yet praise him, who is the health of my countenance, and my God.

You're not going to always have as much energy after chemo, but you will begin to feel stronger a few days after. I didn't even know I wasn't feeling as strong as I used to when my granddaughter Soliel was born. I went to see her shortly after my daughter-in-law gave birth. Soliel weigh about six pounds and maybe three ounces, and she felt very heavy to me, I could only hold her a few minutes. You do have time to get stronger between doctor appointments.

Joshua 1:7–8, NIV
Only be thou strong and very courageous that thou mayest observe to do according to all the law, which Moses my servant commanded thee: turn not from it to the right hand or to the left, that thou mayest prosper whithersoever thou goest.

This book of the law shall not depart out of thou mouth; but thou shalt meditate therein day and night, that thou mayest observe to do according to all that is written therein; for then thou shalt may thy way prosperous, and then thou shalt have good success.

This is spiritual food for your body, but remember there is a saying that you are what you eat. Most parents would go by the food pyramid, and if you're a nutritionist, you will see you don't need as much meat in your diet, and you definitely don't need all the sugar. Sodas and juices have so much sugar in them that are not really good for your immune system. Most doctors don't even have training in nutrition and if you ask them about a plant-based diet, they don't usually don't respond. Try eating more vegetables and see if you feel better. Do this for two weeks, then go back to eating what you usually eat and see how you feel. Listen to your body, it will tell you something's not right, even though you don't know what it is.

We weren't just meant to survive but to thrive. When we hear information that is good for our health, it doesn't hurt to try it. When we give our bodies what it needs, we're telling our bodies that we love ourselves and we want to be good to it. That's why in the Bible it says the body is our temple. Most of us are not really loving ourselves. It's not just food! We work long hours trying to catch up or have more and more. Being in a toxic relationship can affect your health. We have to make choices which help us to maintain our inner peace. Something to do that you do that will help you to get to inner peace. Look at our lives and see if some people are lifting you up or pulling you down. Sometimes it's even people we really love such as family members and our spouses. We have to get a healthy network of support, because we all need each other, but someone toxic in your life will take a negative affect that will show up in your health sooner or later.

The minute you feel anxious, stop what you're doing, and focus on what you're thinking about. Nine times out of ten, it's not even your thoughts. If you're spiritual at all you, will find you need to pull down strongholds that are attacking your mind. Joyce Meyers is the author of *Battlefield of the Mind*. I think she's written several editions. She's even written *Battlefield of the Mind for Teens*. She's a well-known preacher.

We go through a lot of challenges in our life; it actually comes to make us a stronger person, depending on how we perceive it. A lot of our problems are emotional. Our body reacts to situations we're going through. We let other people control our emotions. An example, we could have a boss that's getting on our last nerve, sooner or later that's going to affect you physical. So when you feel pain, you go to the doctor; but when he examines you, he can't find anything wrong. Say for instance you were talking to a friend or a family member and you get upset with them and you may say you make me sick. Well sooner or later you began to feel sick, even though it may take a while but it could be more emotional than physical.

Another thing is that we're harder on ourselves than how we should. I've had problems trying to be perfect, which no one is perfect. Also you need to talk to yourself and tell yourself "God loves me, I love me." Say "I'm going to have a great day, and nobody's going to change that unless I allow them."

When taking chemo, the first thing you usually lose is your hair. It comes out in handfuls. My daughter took me to purchase a wig, and I really wasn't used to wearing wigs, so I really didn't like wearing it. I wouldn't even put it on my head right. So one day I was getting ready for church, I decided I would go to church bald, and I put on a little make-up, and I felt so good about myself. The pastor of my church gave me a compliment on how awesome I looked without the wig. It really made me feel so confident that I didn't put the wig back on my head.

We as women want to look good, and when we lose our hair, it's almost like losing our identity. We take pride in looking good on the outside not really realizing what the put in our bodies will eventually show up on how we look and feel.

We are bombarded by the media with glamorous women looking like models and they look like they work for *Vogue* magazine. So most of us not all try to look like then or try to do our best to look like them. We never stop to think about how much money it took to look like that, they may have the money to buy the food that they need to stay healthy. I don't think they are eating burgers and fries for lunch almost every day. Truth be told, they may be starving themselves to get that body in shape. They may not be stressing over being a single mom working two jobs not knowing how they're going to feed their children from day to day. I'm addressing the women even though I know men are attacked with cancer also. Cancer is not prestige, it attacks black, white, and Chinese, etc.

When I was taking chemo, there were different races, different ages. Cancer is a spirit, and you must war in the spirit to kill it. God has weapons in His armory and we can use them; we have to open our mouths, our mouth is a fierce weapon that can tear down the kingdom of darkness. We have to read the Word of God to educate ourselves. Here are some scriptures you can mediate on and repeat every day. We are strong warriors and we have to let Satan know it.

In our lives we get bombarded with so much, we need to get to a quiet place to hear from God, so we know what decisions that would benefit our lives the most. None of us have all the answers. Only God knows what's best. Every day I wake up grateful to see another sunrise, a breath of fresh air, the scriptures says that His mercy is new every day, also surely His goodness and mercy shall follow me all the days of my life, and I will dwell in the house of the Lord forever. I believe God's spirit dwell in us forever. Even though everything may seem to be working against me, I will cry out to God because He's always behind the seen working for my good. We must realize He's always in control.

Again you need to know that you're loved, you can't push people out of your life when going through treatment. I remember I did because you tend to want people to think you're stronger than you really are. I have a male friend that said he wanted to be there for me; he would call me to encourage me, but he couldn't stand to be in hospitals so he never visited me. I had to forgive him, and that's another thing; when you're sick, you cannot hold any unforgiveness in your heart whether it's family or so-called close friends. Holding unforgiveness is like you drinking poison and waiting for the other person to feel the pain. Most sickness comes from not being able to let go of thoughts that will cause us to be anxious or depressed and even unforgiveness. Forgive and let it go. Check out the movie *Frozen*. You will find out that love wins in the end. So do yourself a favor to let it go, whatever is making you worried or depressed, most of the time we fear something is going to happen that usually never happens.

You have to fight hard not to let having to get treatments affect you. Keep positive thoughts that soon you will be getting better every day.

I've been hearing a lot of doctors that have been doing interviews on the internet that there are new ways of healing cancer. These doctors are looking into options such as how different foods are linked to healing cancer and eliminating cancer cells and also if you have oxygen in your cells, cancer cannot live in your body. That if you have an alkaline diet, not acidic, cancer cannot survive.

Chapter 3

How to Be Your Own Advocate

After your diagnosis, there are more options for treatment than you realize. Have someone that can support you in helping to find a doctor that will give you a second opinion. Please do not let fear take over. When you're faced with such a dilemma, you need to have peace about your decision whether you'll go the chemo or a homeopathic doctor. I know most of us are afraid they we'll make the wrong decisions and we have to make it right away.

My girlfriend told me her sister was a medical doctor for years. After experiencing a brief stay in the hospital, she decided to become a homeopathic doctor. After my girlfriend shared with me about her sister's practice, I decided to make an appointment to see her sister who has a practice in Richmond, Virginia. Her treatment was water and salt in a basin like a whirlpool that you put your feet in to draw out the toxins in your system. I believe it drew most or not all of the toxins out of my system, because the water was very muddy and of different colors. Then I also was given a protein drink, and she prescribed vitamins and supplements.

I wasn't at peace with just this treatment. I decided to go with chemo because I wasn't familiar with homeopathic treatment. I did look online because I heard about a doctor name Lorraine Day, MD, who refused chemo, and she began juicing with carrots, reading the Word of God, and she took supplements. I received all her information, but I realized I didn't have the willpower to go that route. I did know that I couldn't be afraid, the Word of God tells us not to fear. We must trust God in everything we do.

You also must take time to see which route you are going. Just know that if you trust God, He will be with you. He will never leave your nor forsake you. God will take care of you. Many times I had to go in the hospital because my white blood cells were low, they even had to give me a transfusion for two days straight. Also, I was given antibiotics intravenously all week while being hospitalized. You're going to be weak but God will give you strength. Make sure you get a lot of rest. Rest heals your body because while you're sleeping, your cells are renewed.

Three years after taking chemo, this showed up in my email, a documentary about cancer. I missed a lot of the sessions of the speakers expressed that there were alternative methods of treating cancer. The title of the documentary is *The Truth About Cancer*. There is a road less traveled. Some people have such severe reaction to chemo treatments that they can't continue treatments.

So they usually decide to go with vitamins, supplements, and juicing. The reality is our bodies are depleted of most vitamins and minerals we need. Because we are toxic, fasting and drinking lots of water helps us to get rid of a lot of toxins in our bodies. Organic foods should not be taken for granted. It really is not that much more expensive, it's where you usually go to buy your foods. We don't have a taste for really good foods that are good for our health. We often crave for salty foods and foods that are greasy and full of sugar.

In the Bible, in the book of Leviticus, it tells us how to eat and what not to eat. There are many good nutritional books out there. There are many testimonies that people went home and prayed and asked God what to do to help healed their bodies and He spoke to them. One man said God told him to mix many hot peppers to make a tea out of it and after drinking it for a few weeks along with him changing his lifestyle of eating more fruits and vegetables, he began to get well little by little; after going back for his checkup, the doctor said he was getting better and his doctor told him he would be dead in three months without him getting conventional treatment. Another lady said she prayed and God led her to go on vacation to get stress out of her life, she started eating more organic fresh fruits and vegetables, spices, onions, garlic, and juicing raw vegetables. She went hiking in the mountains and became one with nature. She began to feel better. She came back, got checked, and found out she was cancer free. One young man started one round of chemo and he couldn't even walk.

He researched and decided to do a detox cleanse and changed his lifestyle of eating and healthy foods instead of processed foods.

Here are the names of some of the doctors that were interviewed. You can Google the *Truth About Cancer* in your spare time.

Actually one of the persons interviewed that changed his lifestyle of eating also says that cancer is a spirit, and the reason he says it is because it has a lot to do with how and where you are attacked in your body. Also the person who interviewed these doctors had examples of how these patients through prayer were able to get well without chemo; they decided to talk to God believe it or not and they said God gave them the knowledge how to change their lifestyle. Give your life to God start believing in the power of God for your healing. First of all, He created you. So you ask Him what's good for your body. If you have a phone and something is wrong with it, you go to the one who made it.

As you see in the beginning of this book, I had no knowledge; but as time went on, information started showing up. I'm writing this book because I want everyone to know that God is a healer and that in the Word of God, there is hope. There is victory over this disease, and God can and will heal you.

Changing your mind-set is going to be very important. We often can't seem to stay consistent with making eating healthy a part of my existence because our friends, and families aren't changing their eating habits; therefore, we really have to be determined to stay on a lifestyle of eating as healthy as we can. It takes time to do this, but take one day at a time, knowing it's going to help you in the long run. Always ask God to help you because it's His will that you be healthy and that with long life He will satisfy you. We've seen so many friends and family members die from this disease that we often feel like we have no hope but our hope is in Christ Jesus. Our life is hidden in Him, and if He lives in us, and we ask Him to heal us, He is faithful to heal us.

> *And if you ask anything in my name I will do it.*
> *(John 14:14 KJV)*

Chapter 4

Treating Your Body as a Temple

Or do you not know that your body is a temple of the Holy Spirit within you, whom you have from God? You are not your own.
(*1 Cor. 6:19, ESV*)

For ye are bought with a price: therefore glorify God in your body, and in your spirit, which are God's
(*1 Cor. 6:20, KJV*)

So now that we know that we shouldn't just do anything to our bodies to harm our bodies, we need to change our mind-set when we say I'm not hurting anyone but myself when we do anything that will harm our bodies. We're hurting God first and then we're hurting our families and people that love us.

We do it all the time, we're addicts; one of the things we're addicted to is salt and sugar, we think we must have these two substances to flavor our foods when it's not true. There are fresh herbs and spices that make our food taste delicious, but they also have healing properties and we as a nation has not looked research on our own. I didn't do this until I became sick. I had collected a lot of health books, but I looked through them for a while and then I became busy with other things that took my attention, such as work and caring for others. You have to work at trying to keep doing the things that will keep you from stressing out. If you can't afford a vacation go to the park, look at the beautiful flowers and trees, begin to breathe in deeply and let your heart slow down, think about all the wonderful things to be thankful for. Your children are healthy, your wife is healthy, your loved ones are healthy, begin to thank God you have a roof over your head, do something special for someone every day if you have an opportunity. I just want you to know that things are not always as bad as they seem.

We all love a large slice of cake or pie with a large scoop of ice cream, or a large burger and fries; you can enjoy this every now and then, but don't make a habit of eating these foods on a regular basis. Take long walks with your family or love one, one thing I like doing is seeing airplanes take off and land. I like looking in the sky at the clouds. This is a beautiful world, take time to enjoy it. Work will always be here.

When Jesus suffered and died for our sins, the ones we've already committed and the ones we will commit in the futures. He paid the price, He bought us back. He took thirty-nine stripes for our diseases, therefore we have to believe that He wants us well, and if we become sick, He wants to heal us.

> *But he was wounded for our transgressions, he was bruised for our iniquities the chastisement of our peace was upon him; and the chastisement of our peace was upon him; and with his stripes we are sealed.*
> (Isa. 53:5, NIV)

If we can only believe in the Word of God and don't doubt His word and stand on it, as the promise and truth from God. He promised to never leave us nor will He forsake us. He will be with us to the end of the world. That's good to know that He loves us so much and He wants us to love ourselves and others. If you love others, you don't want to see them hurting. Love helps us to be kind to one another. Whatever we do, we have to do it to the glory of God. If we don't know how to pray or what to pray, all we have to do is talk to Father God like you're His child, with all honesty tell Him how you really feel. You should feel like you're able to ask or tell God anything you want or don't understand.

We have to be more conscious of how our bodies feel as a grown up so we can take charge of our lives, so we if we do our part physically and we need God's help spiritually to help us. We need spiritual food as well as natural food.

This is why I'm sharing important scriptures in this book because God wants us to be blessed and living an abundant life. This is what the Holy Scriptures says:

> *This book of the law shall not depart out of thy mouth, but thou shalt meditate therein day and night, that thou mayest observe to do according to all that is written therein: for then thou shalt make thy way prosperous, and then thou shalt have good success. Have not I commanded thee? Be strong and of good courage, be not afraid, neither be thou dismayed: for the LORD thy God Is with thee whithersoever thou goest.*
> (Josh. 1:8–9, KJV)

There are so many different opinions about eating a plant-based diet. One thing I do know is that disease starts in the gut, that there is a second brain in your gut, and that a good cleanse is good for you I believe every six months. And I'm not talking about taking pills, but I do believe the natural way is better such as going to a herbal store and getting herbs and making tea and eating green leafy vegetables and fruits, drinking lots of water at least a gallon, and purify your mind of unhealthy thoughts. The scripture says let this mind be in you which was also in Christ Jesus and we have to take or cast down every argument and every high thing that exalts itself against the knowledge of God. Bring every thought into captivity to the obedience of Christ.

There is an old saying what may be good to you may not always be good for you. People we have to learn to love our bodies as Christ loved us. The FDA may say they're not sure about herbs. But herbs come from God's earth who was created millions and millions of years ago and when He called forth every living creature and all the flowers and plants He called it good. The Bible says the leaves on the trees are good for the healing of the nations and I truly believe God is talking about this earth and not heaven, sometimes we get it wrong.

I believe when you're going through a breakdown in your health, you must turn to God and read and meditate on his word. We need to get to a quiet place, block out all distractions. There is so much going on around us that we have to actually take a deep breath and say this is my time for myself and when we do we have let go of all the thoughts that are not positive, stop worrying about how you're going to pay this hospital bill, let go of what's going to happen to my family, there are so many things we can't control, the Bible says this is not your battle, this war that's going on in your mind is from Satan; he comes to rob, steal, and kill, you can't let him in your mind or heart, keep your mind on Jesus, know that you're not in this alone. I remember Dr. DeSandes said, "Young lady, I don't want you to worry how this bill is going to get paid, focus only on getting well and I took his advice, this journey is not easy, and not everyone going the route of taking chemo and if they go with other methods, it still takes a while to build your immune system, however if God is with you, there can be a suddenly in your life. Your health can turn around and you need to change your lifestyle of what you put in your body. Never give up or give in God is truly a healer."

Most of us grew up on sausage and bacon for breakfast. If you lived on a farm back then it didn't have all the chemical preservatives such as sulfates and nitrates to keep it from spoiling and I believe with these preservatives the meat could not spoil for years, but just know that these chemicals have harmed your cells and are still harming them. Your cells have memory and unless you detoxify your body, at least once a year these toxins are still in your organs, the liver, kidneys, and possibly your heart. All of your organs are vital and play a special part in keeping your healthy. Many, many years ago, the only preservative was salt, and the salt was not processed with all those chemicals.

I suppose because of trying to feed more people, the FDA decided that we needed to do something to preserve food with these harmful chemicals. I say only the strong can survive . . . strong in faith and the spirit of God . . .

The Bible tells us to be strong in the Lord and in the power of his might . . . not our might, we are strong with his power because we can't do anything without him. We're so used to giving into our feelings. Sometimes we feel like we got to have a piece of cake or pie, but then we can't just eat one piece, we have to eat half of it or whatever we're craving, I know I crave sweets, but when they say you have cancer, your need to cancel *all sugar*. We've been told to cut our fats but our brain needs healthy fat like avocado and nuts.

Most of us think we can't afford organic fruits and vegetables, but the doctor office charge much more money for to get us well. We need to know the root cause of disease and it really a combination of things: (1) How do we manage stress. (2) What do we eat. Do you have a stressful job? Do you take time to relax, sit quietly and mediate, do you take a short walk around the block, look at the beautiful flowers and trees, do you take at least nine deep breaths every day . . . I have to remember to do this myself . . . most of us hold things in, we don't really tell people how we really feel for the sake of not hurting someone's feelings, but I believe you can find a way to express yourself without hurting their feelings. You just have to say it in a loving way.

All diseases start at the cellar level. Your body is made up of at least 80 percent of water. Most of us need to drink a lot more water than we do. We substitute water with drinking sodas, tea, coffee and milkshakes, but we say these are liquids also. They may be liquids, but they don't hydrate the body like water does.

At some point in time you have to draw the line in the sand about making bad decisions about how you eat if you love yourself and your temple that God gave you at birth. Sooner or later for some people there will be serious consequences.

This day I call the heavens and the earth
as witnesses against you that
I have set before you life and
death, blessings and curses.
Now choose life, so that
you and your children may live.
(Deut. 30:19 NIV)

You can have a healthy life. It starts by making little changes. Drop off one thing at a time. It starts by making little changes. Try to eliminate fried foods, and if you fall down get back up. Don't be hard on yourself and maybe try to stop eating so many french fries. You really have to listen to your body.

Some people can eat almost anything and not gain weight or not even get sick. I do believe by taking prescriptions will have an adverse effect on your body because there are so many side effects. When you pick up your prescription there are at least two to three pages of what this drug will cause and most say even death. When I get my medication, I say a prayer over it and ask the Holy Spirit not to let any of the side effects harm my body in the name of Jesus.

And yes I've heard that when a journalist have interviewed certain people that have lived to be a ripe age of 95 to 105, and they've said that it have contributed to eating ice cream every day or smoking a cigar every day or other things. I believe these are exceptions and they may have grown up on the farm where they may have not been exposed to harmful chemicals that we're were exposed to and also they may have not had a lot of stress in their lives, which I think most of us have had stress, but it's how you handle it. How we handle life or living our lives in general. We need to know where our food comes from even though we have no jurisdiction, we don't have to purchase it, if we feel like it's to our detriment. We have to be wise and use wisdom. We have to do our own research; no, we may not be a scientist, but we should take time to check out what we are consuming on a daily basis.

Chapter 5

Changing Your Eating Habits

Most of us are not familiar with juicing and smoothies. If you're sixty or over, most of us has a problem in wanting to change. We are stuck in our ways and do not want to change. I can give you some recipes, but it's about time you take the responsibility of your health in your hands, take control of your ability to control the bad habits in your life whatever they may be, but you will need God's help to stay on track, and if you fall down, *"Get back up again, we must feel pain to change."*

I've seen many commercials on how to cure cancer the conventional way or should I say with man-made chemicals. I'm sure it will work for some of us because it worked for me, but I did change from eating less fast foods, boxed foods, and canned foods to more organic foods and organic fruits and vegetables. It's worth it to pay a little more for our food than to end up suffering and in the doctor's office often.

Remember all doctors are not on the same page when it comes to curing diseases. If you're not aware, everything we put in our bodies have positive or negative consequences. We're all not the same genetically, and just because your family member has a disease, it does not mean you do too. It's really what you put in your body that has more effect on you than anything and that even goes for your thoughts and what you think about you.

You can also look up recipes online that are healthy, easy to prepare, and require very little time to prepare. I know we have full schedules, but we have to slow down and realize our health is very important especially if we want to see our sons and daughters graduate from high school and get married. Grandmothers and grandfathers want to experience their grandchildren also.

Because I didn't realize all the information I'm sharing with you until I was told I had cancer. Of course, we all have seen commercials on TV about cancer, but I never thought I would experience it.

I chose chemo because I didn't know my options, and even if you have information you are still afraid to try anything else. I felt like I needed to know more about my options. There is a documentary on the internet titled *The Truth about Cancer*. I suggest you take a look at it. It's by Ty Bollinger. Get educated.

Remember, all doctors are not on the same page when it comes to curing diseases.

Most of us are not familiar with juicing and smoothies. If your sixty or over most of us have a problem of want to change. We are stuck in our ways and do not want to change.

We tend to eat more meat than we should. Meat take a longer time to digest, than most of our foods. When you're on this journey, I suggest that you try curbing your meats, and try to eat more chicken and fish (no canned food). Try not to eat a lot of fried foods also. Drink as much spring water as you can. Nuts are very good, but I suggest you soak them if your teeth can't take it. After soaking, I usually put them in the oven for about ten to fifteen minutes to dry them out.

I suggest you leave sugar alone, such as cakes and pies. If you can't, eat a very thin slice. Cancer cells love sugar. You can add them back later. I also suggest that you begin to make eating wholesome foods as a part of your lifestyle. Most of us crave for sugar in our diet, but we must remember not to go overboard. Sugar is bad for our immune system.

Sometimes when I'm at a restaurant, I may get fries, but very seldom.

Your main concern is to keep a positive attitude and also get in touch with your spirituality, which needs to be fed as well as your natural body. I don't know if you believe in God or what people call your higher self. It's time to reach out to God, begin to communicate with him and your body. He (God) created your body, and he wants you to take care of it. He loves you because you're his child no matter what. We are all his children, and he is very concerned about our wellbeing. We need to get to know him on a deeper level, we need to communicate with him so we can hear his voice. *Again, he loves us. He always has, and he always will.*

Again you need to know that you're loved. You can't push people out of your life when going through treatment. I remember I did because you tend to want people to think you're stronger than you really are. I had a male friend that said he wanted to be there for me. He called up to encourage me, but he never came to see me, so I didn't answer my phone when he called and I had to let it go. And just be thankful that he called. Sometimes it's too much for some people to see you suffering. I had to forgive him.

When you're sick, you cannot hold any unforgiveness in your heart whether it's family or so-called close friends. Holding on to unforgiveness is like drinking poison and waiting for the other person to feel the pain. Stop the pain and forgive; it will benefit your health.

Most sickness comes from not being able to let go of negative thoughts that will cause us to be anxious or depressed. Forgive and move on.

Watch the movie *Frozen*. It's about how powerful love and forgiveness are. So do yourself a favor, let it go, whatever is making you worried or depressed. Most of the time we fear something is going to happen that usually never happens.

You have to fight hard not to let having to get chemo affect you. Keep your thoughts positive every day, and take it one day at a time. Soon you will begin to feel better.

I've been hearing a lot of doctors doing interviews on the internet, informing us that there are new ways of healing cancer. These doctors are looking into options such as how various foods are linked to healing cancer and eliminating cancer cells. Also, they have found that cancer cannot live in an alkaline environment because of the oxygen in our cells. There are certain foods that are considered alkaline foods, and there are foods that are considered acidic. Take some time to explore the alkaline foods for yourself.

The minute you feel anxious, stop what you're doing and focus on what you're thinking about. Nine times out of ten, it's not even your thoughts. If you're spiritual at all, you will find you need to pull down strongholds that are attacking your mind. Joyce Meyer is the author of several books on *Battlefield of the Mind*. I think she's written several editions. She's even written *Battlefield of the Mind for Teens*. She's also a well-known preacher. Reading her books will also give you knowledge on life skills.

We go through a lot of challenges in our life. I believe they actually come to make us a strong person, depending on how we perceive it. A lot of our problems are emotional. Our body reacts to situations we're going through. We let other people control our emotions.

An example, we could have a boss that's getting on our nerves. Sooner or later, that's going to affect you physically. Too much stress on the job or even home can throw off your body chemistry. Stress can affect you in so many ways. Sometimes you can feel pain in your body, and you go to the doctor and he can't find anything wrong, but you know sometimes must be wrong because it's not in your mind.

Sometimes our sickness is more emotional than physical but it appears to be physical. We have to remember to know that while we're going through this journey we have to keep focused on getting well, and not taking on other people's problems.

Taking care of you right now is the most important thing you can do. Worrying about how the hospital bill is going to be paid is none of your concern. The only thing should be on your mind is getting well, and not letting anything get in the way of your health. After you've finished chemo, your job is to continue to get stronger and stronger.

Another thing we're harder on ourselves than anyone else. I've had problems accepting who I was. In my late twenties I was diagnosed as manic which is a type of depression, I was always seeking advice from everyone else instead of trusting my decisions.

I wanted to be perfect and always make the right decision. I never thought I was enough. I procrastinate in making important decision about my life, never thinking I could fit in. Also people use to say you were crazy if you talked to yourself. Well I'm here to tell you that you need to talk to yourself. You need to tell yourself and everyone else that God loves me, I love me and I'm going to have a great day, and nobody's going to change that unless I allow them.

When taking chemo the first thing you usually lose is your hair. It comes out in handfuls.

My daughter took me to purchase a wig and I really wasn't use to wearing wigs, so I really didn't like wearing it. I wouldn't put it on my head right. Sometimes I would put the back of the wig in the front, you can imagine what that looked like. So one day I was getting ready for church, I decided I would go to church bald, and I put on a little make-up and I felt so good about myself, and the pastor of my church gave me a compliment on how awesome I looked with the wig. It really made me feel so confident that I didn't put the wig back on my head when I attended church.

We as women want to look good, and when we lose our hair, it's almost like losing our identity. We take pride in looking good on the outside not really realizing what we put in our bodies will eventually show up on how we look and feel inside. We are bombarded by the media and the glamorous women in Hollywood. We never stop to think about how much money it took to look like that they may have the money to buy the food that they need to stay healthy.

I don't think they are eating burgers and fries for lunch almost every day. Truth be told, they may be starving themselves to get their body in shape. They may not be stressing over being a single mom's working two jobs not knowing how they're going to feed their children from day to day. I'm addressing the women even though I know men are attacked with cancer also. When I was taking chemo, there were different races, different ages.

Cancer is a spirit, and you must war in the spirit to kill it. God has weapons in his armory and we can use them. We have to open our mouths; our mouth is a fierce weapon that can tear down the kingdom of darkness. We have to read the Word of God to educate ourselves.

Food for Thought

Here are some scriptures to meditate on:

Jeremiah 30:17, KJV
For I will restore health unto thee, and I will heal thee of thou wounds, saith the Lord.

Psalm 30:2, KJV
O Lord my God, I cried unto thee, and thou hast healed me.

Psalm 30:3, NIV
O Lord thou hast brought my soul up from the grave; thou hast kept me alive, that I should not go down to the pit.

Psalm 118:17, NIV
I shall not die but live, and declare the works of the Lord.

Nahum 1:9, KJV
He will make an utter end of it. Affliction will not rise up a second time.

Isaiah 53:5, KJV
But he was wounded for our transgressions, he was bruised for our iniquities: the chastisement of our peace was upon him; and with his stripes we are healed.

Psalm 107:19–21, KJV
Then they cried unto the Lord in their trouble, and he saved them out of their distresses.

He sent his word, and healed them, and delivered then from their destructions

Oh that men would praise the Lord for his goodness and for his wonderful works to the children of men.

Deuteronomy 30:19, KJV
I call heaven and earth to record this day against you, that I have set before you life and death, blessings and cursing: therefore choose life, that both thou and thy seed may live.

So now that you know you should choose life, you have the power in you to live, no matter what's attacking your body. You have a choice. Take that choice.

Mark 11:24, KJV
Therefore I say unto you. What things soever ye desire. When we pray believe that ye receive them, and ye receive them, and ye shall have them.

Healing should be the desires of your heart, because I'm sure you want to live, but in a healthy body, soul and spirit.

Isaiah 55:11, KJV
So shall my word be that goeth forth out of my mouth, it shall not return unto me void, but it shall accomplish that.

Scripture to Meditate on Daily

The Book of Prayers and Promises from the Word of God

John 11:14, KJV
Hearing it, Jesus said "this illness is not to end in death, but is for the glory of God, so that through it the Son of God maybe glorified."

John 14:12, KJV
I assure you, the one who believes in the me will himself do the works I do and do greater things than these, for I go to the Father.

John 14:15, NIV
And I will bring about whatsoever you ask in my name so that the Father may be gloried in the Son, I will do whatsoever you ask in My name.

Ephesians 6:11–18, NIV
Put on the complete armor that God supplies, so you will be able to stand against the devil's intrigues. For our wrestling is not against flesh and blood, but against the rules, the authorities the cosmic powers of this present darkness, against the spiritual forces of evil in the heavenly spheres. Take up therefore the whole armor of God, so that you may be able to withstand when you have done all the fighting.

So stand your ground with the belt of truth tightened around your waist wearing the breastplate of righteousness on your body with the readiness of the good news of peace that bound on your feet above all taking up the shield of faith with which you will be able to extinguish all the flaming arrows of the evil one.

And take the helmet of salvation and the sword of the spirit which is the Word of God praying in the spirit on every occasion with ceaseless prayer and entreaty constantly alert to pray with all perseverance and entreaty for all the saints.

Psalm 63:7, KJV
Because you are my help, I sing in the shadow of your wings, my soul clings to you, your right hand upholds me.

Psalm 66:1–2, KJV
Shout with joy to God, all the earth sing the glory of his name; make his praise glorious.

Psalm 67:1, KJV
May God be gracious to us and bless us and make his face shine upon us, Selah.

Psalm 63:7, KJV
Because you are my help, I sing in the shadow of your wings,
My soul clings to you, your right hand upholds me.

Psalm 66:1–2, KJV
Shout with joy to God, make his praise glorious!

Psalm 67:1, NIV
May God be gracious to us and bless us and make his face shine upon us, Selah

Psalm 69:29, NIV
I am in pain and distress, may your salvation O God, protect me.

Psalm 70:1, KJV
Hasten O God, to save me, O Lord, come quickly to help me.

Psalm 92:8, NIV
But you o Lord, are exalted forever. He shall have dominion also from sea to sea and from the river unto the ends of the earth.

Psalm 92:1–2, KJV
It is good to praise the Lord and make music to your name, O most high. To proclaim your love in the morning and your faithfulness at night, o the music of the ten stringed lyre and the melody of the harp.

Psalm 119:11, KJV
I have hidden your word in my heart that I might not sin against you.

Psalm 119:14–20, KJV
I rejoice in following your statutes as one rejoice in great riches.
I meditate on your precepts and consider your ways.
I delight in your decrees; I will not neglect your word.
Open my eyes that I may see wonderful things in your law.
I am a stranger on earth; don't hide your commands from me.
My soul is consumed with longing for your laws at all times.

Psalm 94:22, KJV
But the Lord has become my fortress and my God the rocks whom I take refuge.

Psalm 97:6, KJV
The heavens proclaim his righteousness and all the peoples see his glory.

Psalm 102:1–2, NIV
Hear my prayer O Lord, let the cry for help come to you. Do not hide your face from me when I am in distress. Turn your ear to me; when I call answer me quickly.

I Kings 8:22, NIV
O Lord, God of Israel, there is no God like you in the heaven above or on earth below. You keep your covenant of love with your servants who continue wholeheartedly in your way.

I Kings: 8:28, KJV
But will God really dwell on earth? The heavens, even the highest heavens, cannot contain you.

I Chronicles 17:20, 23, KJV
There is no one like you, O Lord and there is no God but you, as we have heard with our own ears.

And now, Lord, le the promise you have made concerning your servant and his house be established forever. Do as you promised, so that it will be established and that your name will be great forever. Then men will say, the Lord Almighty, the God over Israel, is Israel's God!

Psalm 63:1, KJV
O God, you are my God, earnestly I seek you, my soul thirst for you; in a dry and weary land where there is no water.

Psalm 63:3, KJV
Because your love is better than life, my lips will glorify you.

Psalm 63:4, KJV
I will praise you as long as I live, and in your name I will lift up my hands,

Psalm 63:5, NIV
My soul will be satisfied as with the richest of foods; with singing lips my mouth will praise you.

Job 36:5, KJV
God is mighty, but does not despise men, he is mighty and firm in his purpose.

Job: 6, KJV
He does not take his eyes off the righteous, he enthrones them with Kings and exalts them forever.

Job: 11, NIV
If they obey and serve him, they will spend the rest of their days in prosperity and their years in contentment.

Job: 12, NIV
But if they do not listen, they will perish by the sword and die without knowledge

Psalm 8:1, NIV
O Lord our Lord how majestic is your name in all the earth.

Psalm 11:4, KJV
The Lord is in his Holy temple, the Lord is on his heavenly throne.

Psalm 16:1 KJV
O Lord thou hast brought my soul up from the grave; thou hast kept me alive, that I should not go down to the pit.

Psalm 118:17, KJV
I shall not die but live, and declare the works of the Lord.

Nahum 1:9, KJV
He will make an utter end of it. Affliction will not rise up a second time.

Isaiah 53:5, KJV
But he was wounded for our transgressions, he was bruised for our iniquities: the chastisement of our peace was upon him; and with his stripes we are healed.

Psalm 107:19–21, NIV
Then they cried unto the Lord in their trouble, and he saved them out of their distresses.

He sent his word, and healed them, and delivered then from their destructions Oh that men would praise the Lord for his goodness and for his wonderful works to the children of men

Psalm 91:10–16, KJV
There shall no evil befall thee, neither shall any plague come nigh they dwelling,

For he shall give his angels charge over thee, to keep thee in all thy ways.

They shall bear thee up in their hands, lest thy dash thy foot against a stone.

Thou shall tread upon the lion and adder: the young lion and the dragon shalt thou trample under feet.

Because he hath set his love upon me, therefore will I deliver him; I will set him on high, because he hath known my name.

He shall call upon me, and I will answer him; I will deliver him, and honour him

With long life will I satisfy him, and shew him my salvation.

Printed in the United States
By Bookmasters